POETRY HIDES

SOPHIA MCCRAY

EDITED BY
NICOLE QUEEN

CONTENTS

PREFACE

Over the past several years, I've experienced many life-changing experiences that have afforded me the opportunity to learn valuable wisdom. Poetry Hides is the beginning of my testimony, conveyed through the art of poetic expression. It is a collection of my personal experiences, containing moments of pain, memories, and lessons learned. But most importantly, it affirmatively points to the revelation of God's grace.

Because of God's grace, I have been afforded this distinct opportunity to share my story; He has blessed me with the strength to write. I am thankful for your time and dedication to embracing this journey with me. Your support conveys your faith in the presence of God in me. For that, I am humbled and honored for the opportunity to share a brief snapshot of my life and experiences with you. May you be blessed by the revelation of God's grace!

A VACATION

A vacation goes without hesitation
A fun and exciting situation
Filled with laughter fun and games
Once it's over things will never be the same
Spending money without a care
Spending money with delay of fear
Don't forget the bills and monthly debts
Try to have fun without regrets
I bet the next vacation will begin with hesitation
Just so you won't return to frustration

GRADE 4

I am tired
I simply cannot shout anymore
All because of
The children in Grade 4
They never listen
To a word I say
All they do
Is sit and play
I tried to be strong
And speak very stern
I think they forgot
They came here to learn
There is one thing
I forgot to mention
This class will definitely
Have a lunchtime detention
It will go on every day

Until they settle down
And stop acting like
Doubles of Bobo the Clown
Maybe tomorrow
They will all start anew
Come to school to learn
Like they are supposed to
No matter what
I'll show up each day
To set the tone
And show them the way
I know that fine day
Soon will arrive
When they will go on
To the next Grade 5
And when the school year
Is about to begin
I'll get this poem out
And start over again

LIFE

As tall as a ship
As big as a house
As loud as a helicopter
As quiet as a mouse
As rough as the seas
On a stormy winter's night
As calm as a placid lake
Through winter's first sight
As red as an apple
As round as the sun
To find the hidden treasure
Life has just begun

FAMILY

Families are special
Families are fun
Families build children
Into the people they become
They hold your hand
When times are tough
They give you a lift
When the road gets rough
Families are lifesavers
A round circle treat
Everyone's family
Is different and unique

DEPTH

To feel empty in your soul
To feel empty in your heart
To have your whole world
Torn apart
It's amazing what you see
As life passes you by
The shapes and the colors
You see in the sky
Standing there alone
Standing as still as stone
Wondering why to yourself
Just those pictures left on the shelf
Remembering the good and the bad
The happy and the sad
Always thinking you were fine
Never thinking I'd run out of time

The special things you always did
Doing things you know I'd forbid
As you lived your life through
Never forget— I love you

Am I In Love?

It passes over me
Like a gentle breeze
I give into its pleasures
With oh such ease
I sit on the riverbank
Watch the stars above
I sit and wonder
Am I in love
It was all so sudden
These feelings I treasure
Feelings of delight
Extreme pleasure
To feel wanted and needed
From a man who exceeded
My dreams, my passions
In an ordinary fashion
It passes over me

Like a gentle breeze
I give into its pleasures
With oh such ease
I sit on the riverbank
Watch the stars above
I sit and wonder
Am I in love

HUNGRY?

The rattle of the pots
The rattle of the pans
The sound of the water running
As I wash my hands
The sound of the knife chopping
Slicing onions and peppers
The whistle of the pot
Such a simmering sound
The aroma fills the air
Making my stomach grumpy
Ummm
I am hungry

I Wonder

Sometimes I wonder
Where I've been
Who I am
Do I fit in
Sometimes I wonder
As I wander by
What is the color
Of the sky
Some say orange
Others say blue
I haven't seen it
Tell me— have you
Seen all of life's gifts
From God up above
All of life's gifts
I'm encouraged to love
So as I wonder

As life passes me by
I can only imagine
The color of the sky
Make no mistake
It's easy to see
A world created for you
And for me
But for some reason
I cannot find
The answer to the question
Why am I blind

ICE CREAM

Wet
Cold
Dripping down my hand
Melting in the sun
Drip, drop, drip, drop
Catching the flavors
As the race begins
Tasting just a smudge
Swiftly as it runs
Across my taste buds
Sliding, gliding
Down my throat
Savoring the taste
Before it's over

INTERPRETATION

To set your mind free—
Music
Let your spirit soar—
Music
To feel the rhythm in your heart—
Music
To never feel alone—
Music

KIDS

Kids are the funniest
People on earth
Looking, searching
For their self-worth
Plenty of hugs
Plenty of kisses
Plenty of time
To fulfill all their wishes
To listen, to share
A definite must
To reach them in depth
To secure them in trust
To educate, to demonstrate
To advise, to conduct
Kids— a live volcano
Ready to erupt

MEMORIES

I can remember our very first kiss
To feel your gentle press upon my lips
To feel your gentle hands upon my face
Made my heart immediately race
For no one has ever made me feel
A love so gentle, a love so real
We met on a bright, sunny day
What drew us together, I could not say
As our eyes met, so did our hearts
We didn't know what was about to start
Our life together, till death do us part
When I look into your eyes, I see my best friend
A strong solid, wonderful man
Loyalty, trust, and love to withstand
I see inside the windows of your soul
All these things I feel
Upon your strong, but gentle hold

So as I sit, I dream about our first kiss
I close my eyes and think of this
Your heart so sweet, your heart so pure
I long for the moment you walk through the door
To hold me in your arms— so secure so tight
Hold me in your arms for the rest of the night

MOTHERHOOD

Moms are special
Moms are fun
A mom is someone
That I've become
To love, to nurture
A challenge for some
Stand up to the test
The games have just begun
To hold their hand
To guide them through
Whatever you do
Don't forget to say 'I love you'
A simple phrase
So many wish to hear
A simple phrase
It's music to their ears
So once they're grown

And ready to leave the nest
Trust in them
Believe you did your best
The memories you share
Will take you through and through
There's one thing left to do
Say 'I love you'

MUSIC

Music is a universal voice
Everyone can listen to with choice
To choose how they interpret the musical sound
With each note, they become spellbound
It makes you happy; it makes you sad
It makes you wonder about things you never had
Why wonder; just set the bar
Be that bright, shining star

REVELATION

It's strange how many desire
A friendship like ours, that amazingly transpired
Only through talk, never of sight
Only conversations of pure delight
Delights and pleasures, wanting you by my side
Consulting and confiding the things we thought we'd hide
Guiding each other, a new task for two
This is a friendship for me— is it for you?
I guess these words just go to say
This friendship that will never go away

SHOES

Have you heard
The latest news
It's the blues
All about shoes
Shoe, shoes
They're so neat
You must wear shoes
To protect your feet
Some have heels
Some are flat
They're the best
To protect your back
Brown ones, black ones
Reds ones, too
I have thirty pairs
How about you?
Lace up, buckles

Slip-ins and boots
To stay in style
Go back to your roots
In the end
Without despair
It doesn't matter
What you wear
Work your stride
Show your glory
Shoes can tell
Your whole life story

.

STRENGTH

Never give up
Never give in
Never let the devil win
You've got heart
You've got a choice
Open up and rejoice
Be the one
Don't you stop
You can make it to the top
Think you can
You're almost there
Hold up your head and persevere
Use good judgment
The devil is a fraud
Open up your heart and listen to God

THE ALMIGHTY

The sound of the wind
The feel of the sand
The essence of sound
Leaves you spellbound
The sound of the night
A baby's first flight
These precious first
Leaves you in pure delight
Deep as the ocean
Deep as the soul
Leaves the mysteries of life
Yet to unfold
The revelation
Of what's to become
The path of one's life
God's gift to everyone
Sit, relax

Let Him drive you
In the right direction
A life of true perfection
This is a reflection
Of your trust in God

LOVE OF MY LIFE

Just think what we've
Become together
Some people only dream
Of a love so pure
For quite a while
I couldn't understand
The blessings I received
From this wonderful man
He gives me flowers
He holds me tight
He makes me laugh
He treats me right
Such warm feelings
Of pure delight
Precious moments
By candlelight
The time has come for us to show

The world our love
To show the beauty
That love can truly be
The love that transpired
Between you and me
The love so many
Refuse to see
To show the world
What's to come
The love we can share
Together as one
I'm so thankful
I have you in my life
To stand beside you
To fight all the strife
To be true, our love
We will never part
'I love you, God'
From the bottom of my heart

The Rain

The rain
Let it embrace you
The rain
Rhythmic massaging drops
The rain
It captures you, as only an audience should be
The rain
Music to your ears
The rain
My private band on my roof at night

LISTEN

How do we listen
To listen with your ears is just to take in
But not to understand
To listen with your heart is to listen
Without rational understanding
To listen with your mind is to listen
With reason, with full comprehension
And without judgment
To listen with your soul is to listen
With an open mind
To gain a spiritual connection
Without boundaries
Allow you inner self
To trust and be trusted
How do you listen

Unrequited Love

Eye spy my little raisin eyes
The wind is churning
My heart's a-burnin'
It's as hot as the touch of ice
But I'm still frozen
An endless circle
Of never ending obstacles
Standing at the foot of a mountain
I see only shadows
But I'm still frozen
The buzzing sounds inside my head
The whoosh of thoughts
That go unsaid
The cracking of a broken heart
But I'm still frozen

WORDS

What is in a word
What can words do
How you interpret
It's up to you
One word
Many meanings
One might say words
Are so misleading
Words can hurt, hinder, or soothe
It's how you say them
That molds emotions into actions
Actions that become reactions
All are matters of the heart
They remain unseen until
Words help people manifest
Who we truly are

Words at rest
Until they put us to the test
Words, so simple
Who would have thought

CHANGE

Do you ever wonder
Why change is a part of life
In order to grow
One must experience anger, strife
How to move in the world
Is a lesson we all need
To enhance our future
We must all take heed
Listen to the old
Their experience is true
If you listen with your soul
You'll know just what to do
So, as you wander through life
And things seem strange
Just remember life's lesson
It's all about change

CROSSING THE STREET

Look to the left
Look to the right
Check the area
Before stepping into sight
Make sure it's safe
Get up the nerve
Before you step
Right off that curb
Red means stop
Yellow means ready
Don't walk on green
The cars will squash you like spaghetti
Before you cross
Check out the lights
And always remember
Look left, look right

I Want To Go Home

I want to go home
I want to go home
It's lonely here
I want to go home
Where there's family and friends
I want to go home
Where there's love and happiness
I want to go home
Where the aroma is just right
I want to go home
Do you know the way

LAY THEM DOWN

Stranger things have happened
Brighter days will come
No matter what the situation
Always turn to someone
Someone whom you trust
Confide in them you must
Release, so not to become distraught
You can always confide in God
He always listening
Even when you think he's not
He'll deliver when He's ready
When you thought he had forgot
So remember when you struggle
Or even when you don't
Just talk to him, He'll listen
Even when others won't

SOLEMN VOW

Today, as we stand here before God
I pledge my love to you
For there has never been a love
So pure as you
From this day forward
I will honor you
Stand by you
Care for you
In sickness and in health
As we take this step together
As man and wife
I pledge to love you
Cherish each day with you
For the rest of my life
This is my solemn vow

Numbers

Where do they come from
Where do they end
Many needs for them
To help us understand
To measure in time
Distance and space
Don't second guess
You're right on the case
You're right on the path
You'll be a hero
Start counting now
Starting from zero

OUR GREEN EARTH

A field of green
Damp with morning dew
The colors of spring
Bright, fresh, and new
Nature's conversation
Warms you with delight
Invades your heart
Like love at first sight
The five senses you get
All given at birth
To explore and enjoy
On our green earth

PLACID

To watch the sunrise
On our beautiful island
To watch the ripple of the water
As the still winds blow
To listen to the crickets
As they sing in the night
Calms the soul
Sounds of pure delight
To find the simple things
That make life all it's worth
You'll find it here on
Our green earth

Rain

Drip drop, slip slop
Listen to the rain plop
Taping on your window pane
Mother Nature sounds again
Listen to the funky beat
Pitter patter stomp your feet
Close your eyes and fade away
Pray to God that come what may
One, two, three, four, five
Open your sleepy eyes
Listen to the songs of rain
Mother Nature sounds again

JUST FOR ME

Let us give thanks to the Lord
Yes, He's the One
He gave His only begotten Son
Just gave Him to us with open arms
Without a care and with all His charm
To stand beside us through the fight
To hold us close throughout our plight
The pain He felt, where should I begin
He died for us; forgave all our sins
So we could live and praise His Name
Our lives will never be the same
The sacrifice was made with no hesitation
So we could live in conservation
So many things to try and explain
Stop and read the Bible to obtain
Knowledge, wisdom

There's so much to gain
Just be glad Jesus died and rose again

POETRY HIDES

Poetry hides
In my son's morning voice
Poetry hides
In my husband's playful energy
Poetry hides
In the sound of 'I love you'
Poetry hides
In the rattle of the pots and pans
Poetry hides
In the thunder of running water
Poetry hides
In the quiet sound of sleep
Poetry hides
In the sound of the night
Poetry hides
In everyday life

When You Believe

Follow your heart
Even when skies are gray
Follow your heart
No matter what people may say
Believe in yourself
No matter what the task may be
Believe in yourself
No matter what your eyes may see
Trust in God
You know His love is true
Trust in God
He's the only One who can bring you through

FAITH

Faith is something you walk with
Faith is something you can strengthen with God
Faith is something you can build on
Faith is something that personal— it's yours
Faith is something to always have on your side
Faith is something, when if you let it can strengthen you
Faith is something that you can trust always
Faith is something you should have in order to win
With God on your side, you always win

THE STORY

Lessons we learn in life each day
Build a path to show us the way
If we listen closely, we must take heed
In order to grow in life and succeed
Gifts so freely, given by God
So many take for granted, despite what's been taught
The lessons of life are in print and bold
Turn to the Bible and get life's story retold
The knowledge and power you'll get— it's true
Let the Word of Bod bestow upon you

NEW BEGINNINGS

A new year
A new start
Set high goals
Begin with your heart
To some
It may sound strange
But no matter what
You decide to change
Begin anew
The change should start
And begin with you
Some change for others
But mostly for self
Make a growth chart
Plan for prosperity and wealth
So when you step back

And see your life at a glance
Don't give up now
Give life a second chance

THE JOY OF CHRISTMAS

Christmas time is full of fun
Toys and gifts for everyone
Full of love and lots to share
Time to show so many you care
The hustle and bustle of people in the stores
Excited to spend money more and more
Bringing happiness to so many we know
Looking out the window and hoping for snow
Enjoying the sounds and smell that Christmas brings
Listening and enjoying the carolers sing
When it's all over and said and done
The new year's the beginning
And life has just begun

God Is Watching

God is watching over me and over you
God is watching even when we don't know what to do
If you trust and believe in the power of prayer
Get on your knees and take it there
Give it to Him; He wants it all
Give it to Him; He'll hear your call
So when you're feeling down and out
And your heart is full of doubt
Trouble will come knocking
Always remember God is watching

ALL WET

Pitter-patter
Splash and splatter
On my window pane
Pitter-patter
Splash and splatter
Here comes the pouring rain
Bolts of lightning
Crash of thunder
Hear that spooky sound
Pitter-patter
Splash and splatter
Puddles on the ground

OUR FATHER

God—
Gracious, omnipotent, divine
Father to us all
Will never leave us when we fall
God—
Generous, obedient, deliverer
Giver of all things, precious and true
Maker of destinies for me and for you
Always there
In your time of need
You don't have to beg
You don't have to plead
Just open your heart
He sees right through
Give it to Him
He'll know what to do
Stand and believe

Prayer is what's best
The Bible has answers
To put it all to rest
So in times of worry
And in times of fear
Count on God
He's standing right there

TIME

Tick, tock
Tick, tock
Counting numbers on the clock
How many hands do I see
Short and long
There's 2 by me
Count by 5's
Count by 10's
Up to 60 and back again
Start at 8; finish at 3
Lunch in the middle
And time for tea
Before you know it
Our day is done
Counting numbers is so much fun

CANDY!

I'm so hungry; what should I eat
Candy, candy— oh, so sweet
Bubble gum, jelly beans, and gumdrops
Oh, please can I have the big lollipop
Snickers, Butterfinger, Skittles, and more
I just can't wait to go to the store
The corner market is the place to be
To spend my $5 on pure candy
At the store, I'm never forgotten
All this candy's gonna make my teeth rotten
That's alright, cause I'm about to chill
My mom just got my dentist bill

BIG BROTHERS

Big brothers are fun
Big brothers are smart
Big brothers teach you all about art
They hold your hand
In the dark at night
They're the ones
Who hold the flash light
Share their food
Put a smile on your face
No one can ever take their place
So when times are tough
And there's no other
I can always count on my big brother

BIG SISTERS

Big sisters are funny
They talk about boys
They don't have any real big toys
Shout, 'Don't touch my stuff'
And 'Leave me alone'
And always on the telephone
Writing in journals
Reading girly books
Putting makeup on to perfect their looks
When she goes to college
I'm really going to miss her
Because I truly love my big sister

PERSONAL STORMS

Every day is not a good day; feeling full of doubt
Trapped inside, hearing myself shout
Shouting for help, only no one can hear
Suddenly realizing my own biggest fear
Suffocated by the pain of depression
Scared by my own sense of aggression
Drowning in fear, worry, and pain
Wondering if life will ever be the same
Learning how to accept what is, not what was
Holding on for dear life, only because
It's a gift of burrow, and not yours to own
A destiny God has given, His love He has shown
When you feel trapped, alone and in despair
Give it to God, He will be there
Seek His comfort, He believes in you
Give it to Him, He will see you through

I Am A Woman

Strong, proud, and confident
Who am I ... a woman
Smart, sexy, cultured, and witty
Who am I... a woman
Challenged by society, defined by shape
Who am I... a woman
Often misunderstood and misrepresented
Who am I... a woman
Single parent, beating the odds
Who am I... a woman
Setting the bar and demanding respect
Who are we... women

MY FRIEND

Playing catch with the sun
Running through the shadows
Trying not to get caught
She reaches through the tree branches
Trying to catch me as I run
Dodging the opportunity to be played
By her brilliant shining rays
Staying in the safe zones
Catching my breath, staying cool
Having fun until dusk
Tomorrow, playing is a must
My friend always comes out to play
Unless the rain chases her away

ABOUT THE AUTHOR

 Sophia McCray is native-born to the island of Bermuda. She now lives in Maryland and has a passion for writing and music. Sophia is a mom of two boys. She uses her personal life experiences to make her writing come alive. Living on faith and the Word of God, Sophia believes that transparency is the key to becoming a successful writer.